XTREME UNIVERSE

SUPERNOVAS

AND MORE SIZZLING SIGHTS

A&D Xtreme
BOLD HI-LO NONFICTION
An imprint of Abdo Publishing
abdobooks.com

ANN WILLIAMS

TAKE IT TO THE XTREME!

GET READY FOR AN EXTREME ADVENTURE! THE PAGES OF THIS BOOK WILL TAKE YOU INTO THE THRILLING WORLD OF ASTRONOMICAL WONDERS. WHEN YOU HAVE FINISHED READING THIS BOOK, TAKE THE XTREME CHALLENGE ON PAGE 45 ABOUT WHAT YOU'VE LEARNED!

ABDOBOOKS.COM
Published by Abdo Publishing, a division of ABDO, PO Box 398166, Minneapolis, Minnesota 55439.

Printed in the United States of America, North Mankato, MN.
102024
012025

THIS BOOK CONTAINS RECYCLED MATERIALS

Design: Kelly Doudna, Mighty Media, Inc.
Production: Mighty Media, Inc.
Editor: Katherine Chu

Cover Photograph: NASA/ESA/ASU/J. Hester
Interior Photographs: ALMA (ESO/NAOJ/NRAO)/M. Maercker et al., pp. 12–13; Angel DiBilio/Shutterstock Images, pp. 30–31; Brookhaven National Laboratory/Flickr, pp. 34–35; Chandra X-ray Observatory Center/NASA/CXC/NCSU/M.Burkey et al (X-ray), DSS (Optical), pp. 18–19; CTIO/NOIRLab/DOE/NSF/AURA, pp. 6–7; ESA/Hubble & NASA, pp. 32–33; ESA/Hubble & NASA/Acknowledgment: Judy Schmidt, pp. 24–25; ESA/Hubble & NASA/Acknowledgment: Mahdi Zamani, pp. 20–21; ESO/L. Calçada, pp. 8–9; Hertzog, Samuel Joseph/CERN, pp. 38–39; NASA, pp. 42–43; NASA, ESA and STScI, pp. 26–27; NASA/ESA/ASU/J. Hester, p. 1; NASA, ESA, CSA, pp. 36–37; NASA, ESA, CSA, D. Milisavljevic (Purdue University), T. Temim (Princeton University), I. De Looze (UGent), J. DePasquale (STScI), p. 44; NASA, ESA, G. Dubner (IAFE, CONICET-University of Buenos Aires) et al.; A. Loll et al.; T. Temim et al.; F. Seward et al.; VLA/NRAO/AUI/NSF; Chandra/CXC; Spitzer/JPL-Caltech; XMM-Newton/ESA; and Hubble/STScI, pp. 10–11; NASA, ESA/Hubble and the Hubble Heritage Team, pp. 14–15; NASA/ESA/JPL-Caltech/UCLA/CXC/SAO, pp. 28–29; NASA/JPL-Caltech/GSFC/JAXA, pp. 16–17; NOIRLab/NSF/AURA/J. da Silva/Spaceengine, pp. 22–23; NRAO/AUI/NSF/GBT/VLA/Dyer, Maddalena & Cornwell (Radio); Chandra X-ray Observatory/NASA/CXC/Rutgers/G. Cassam-Chenaï, J. Hughes et al. (X-ray); 0.9-metre Curtis Schmidt optical telescope/NOAO/AURA/NSF/CTIO/Middlebury College/F. Winkler and Digitized Sky Survey (Visible light), pp. 4–5; Rost9/Shutterstock Images, pp. 40–41
Design Elements: Arafat/Adobe Stock (header background); pixel/Adobe Stock (universe); Sergey Nivens/Shutterstock Images (header background)

LIBRARY OF CONGRESS CONTROL NUMBER: 2024938302
PUBLISHER'S CATALOGING-IN-PUBLICATION DATA
Names: Williams, Ann, author.
Title: Supernovas and more sizzling sights / by Ann Williams
Description: Minneapolis, Minnesota : ABDO Publishing, 2025 | Series: Xtreme universe | Includes online resources and index.
Identifiers: ISBN 9781098295080 (lib. bdg.) | ISBN 9798384915133 (ebook)
Subjects: LCSH: Supernovas--Juvenile literature. | Stars--Juvenile literature. | Stars, Brightest--Juvenile literature. | Universe--Juvenile literature. | Outer space--Exploration--Juvenile literature. | Astronomy--Juvenile literature.
Classification: DDC 523.112--dc23

CONTENTS

CHAPTER 1

A FLASH IN THE NIGHT SKY

You're on a family camping trip at a state park. You brought your telescope so you can stargaze away from the lights of the city. As you scan the night sky, you see a particularly large, bright star. You may have spotted one of the hottest objects in the universe—a supernova!

SN 1006 is one of the brightest supernovas ever recorded.

CHAPTER 2

WHAT IS A SUPERNOVA?

When a **massive** star explodes, it's called a supernova. A star's center is made of gases held together by gravity. These gases are constantly burning and getting hotter. Massive stars burn large amounts of gas. This creates lots of energy that presses outward. Meanwhile, gravity continuously presses inward.

The Vela supernova remnant. A supernova remnant is what remains after a star explodes.

Eventually, the star runs out of gas to burn. So, it starts to cool. The outward energy isn't as strong as the gravity pressing inward. This makes the star **collapse** suddenly. The collapse is very fast and strong. It causes a huge explosion, or a supernova.

The temperature in a supernova can reach 180 billion degrees Fahrenheit (100 billion°C)!

CHAPTER 3

FROM NEBULA TO RED GIANT

A star's life consists of several stages. It starts as a large cloud of dust and **hydrogen** gas. This cloud is called a nebula. Gravity pulls the gas together, causing it to spin and clump.

As it clumps, the gas's atoms start to **collide**. This causes the gas to get hot. Once the gas is hot enough, the nebula's center starts to glow and becomes a protostar.

One of the brightest supernova remnants is the Crab Nebula. Some nebulas are created from a supernova's leftover gas and dust.

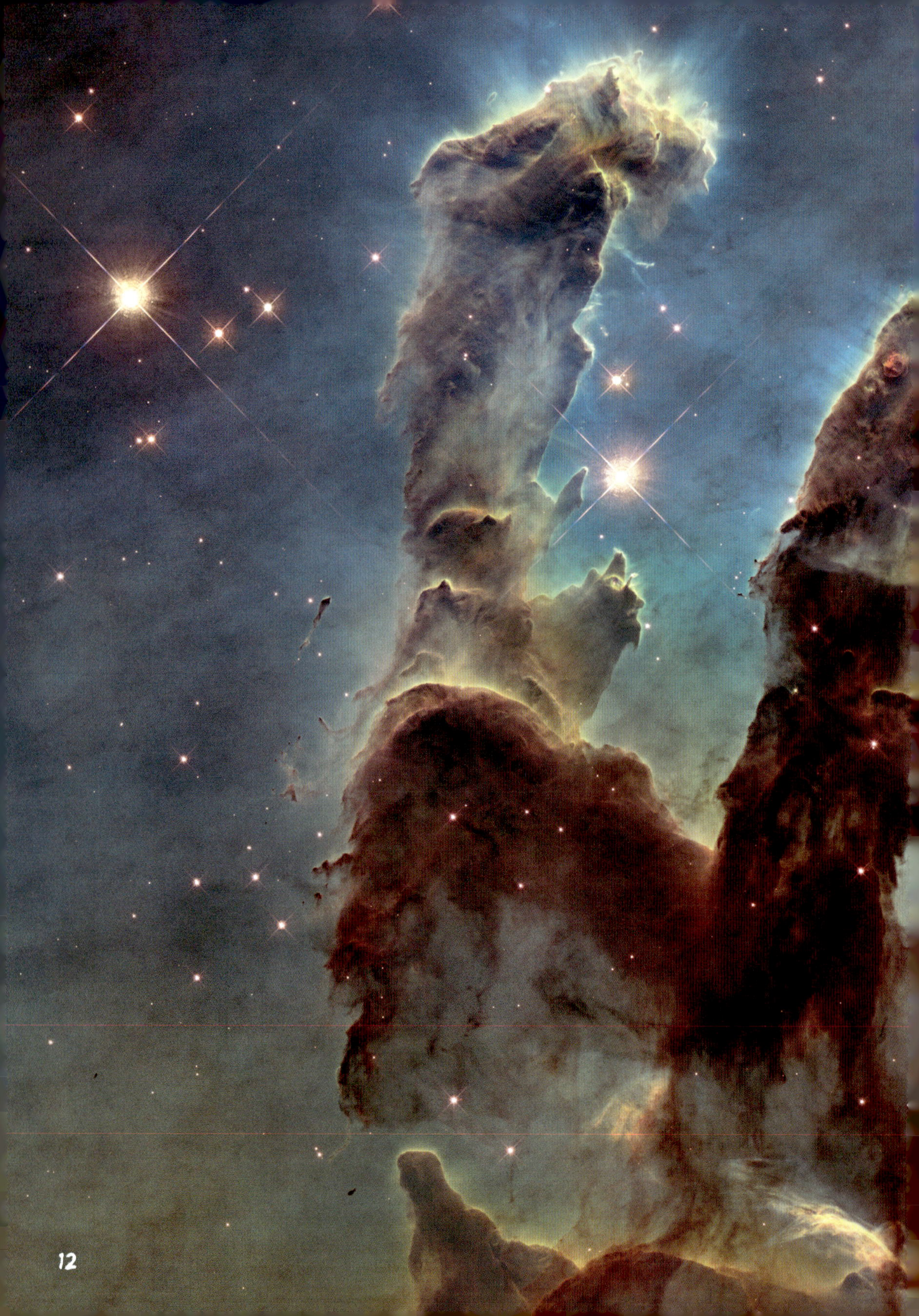

The protostar continues to gather matter from the nebula. This makes the protostar grow bigger. It stops growing when there isn't any matter left in the nebula. It is now a main sequence star. This is usually the longest stage of a star's life.

The Eagle Nebula. Scientists sometimes call nebulas "star nurseries." This is because they contain multiple stars that are starting to form.

During the main sequence star stage, gravity and heat are constantly causing a **reaction** in the star's **core**. This reaction is called nuclear fusion. Eventually, this causes the core to become unstable and start to contract.

Meanwhile, the star's **outer** shell starts to move outward and cool. As the shell cools, it starts to glow red. The star is now a red giant.

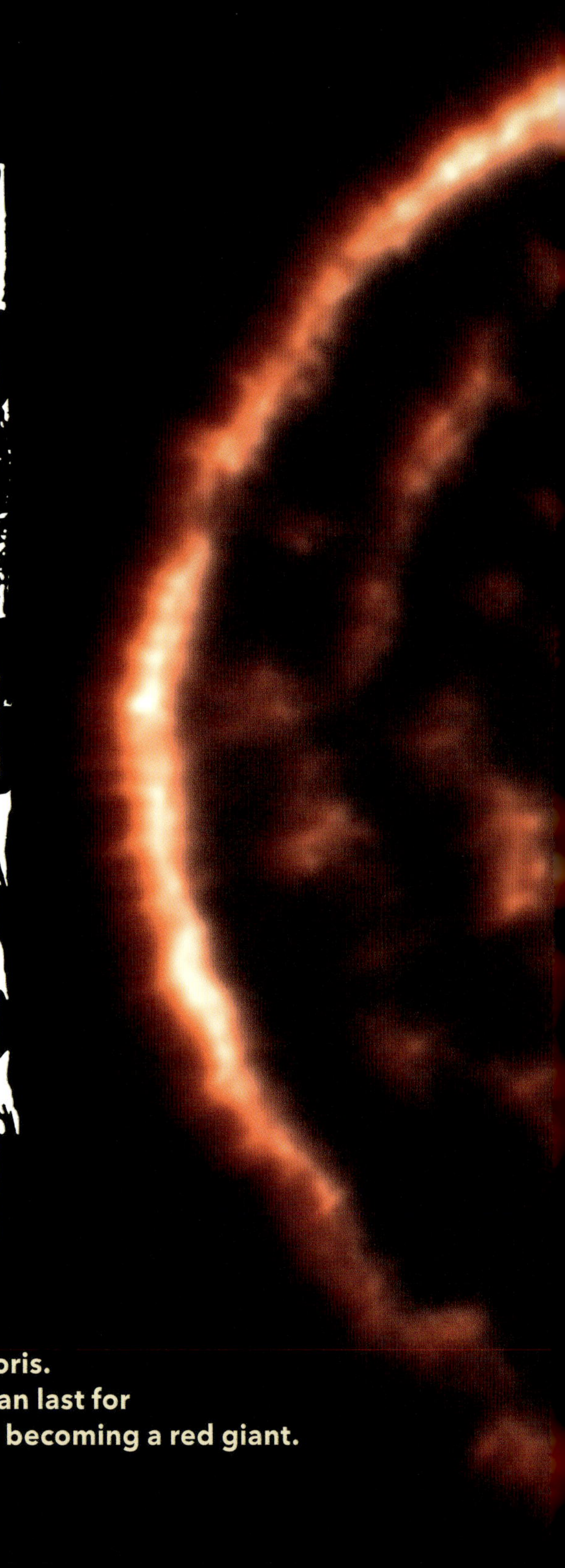

Red giant star R Sculptoris.
A main sequence star can last for billions of years before becoming a red giant.

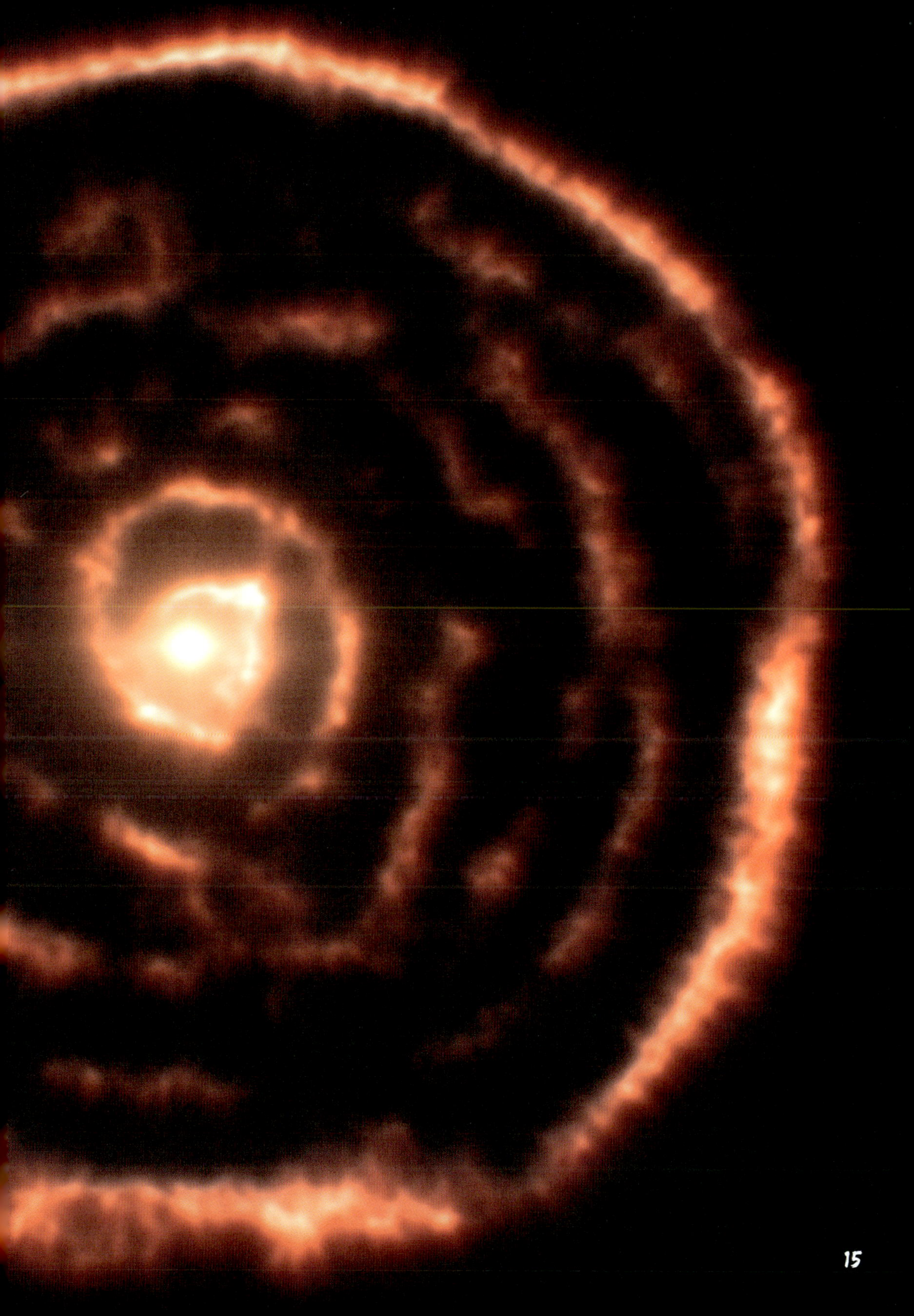

CHAPTER 4

RED GIANTS AND BEYOND

All stars become red giants the same way. What happens after that depends on the size of the star. A small to medium star slowly cools, becoming a white dwarf. When all its energy is gone, the star becomes a black dwarf.

The sun is a main sequence star. It is about 4.6 billion years old! Scientists believe it will become a white dwarf in several billion years.

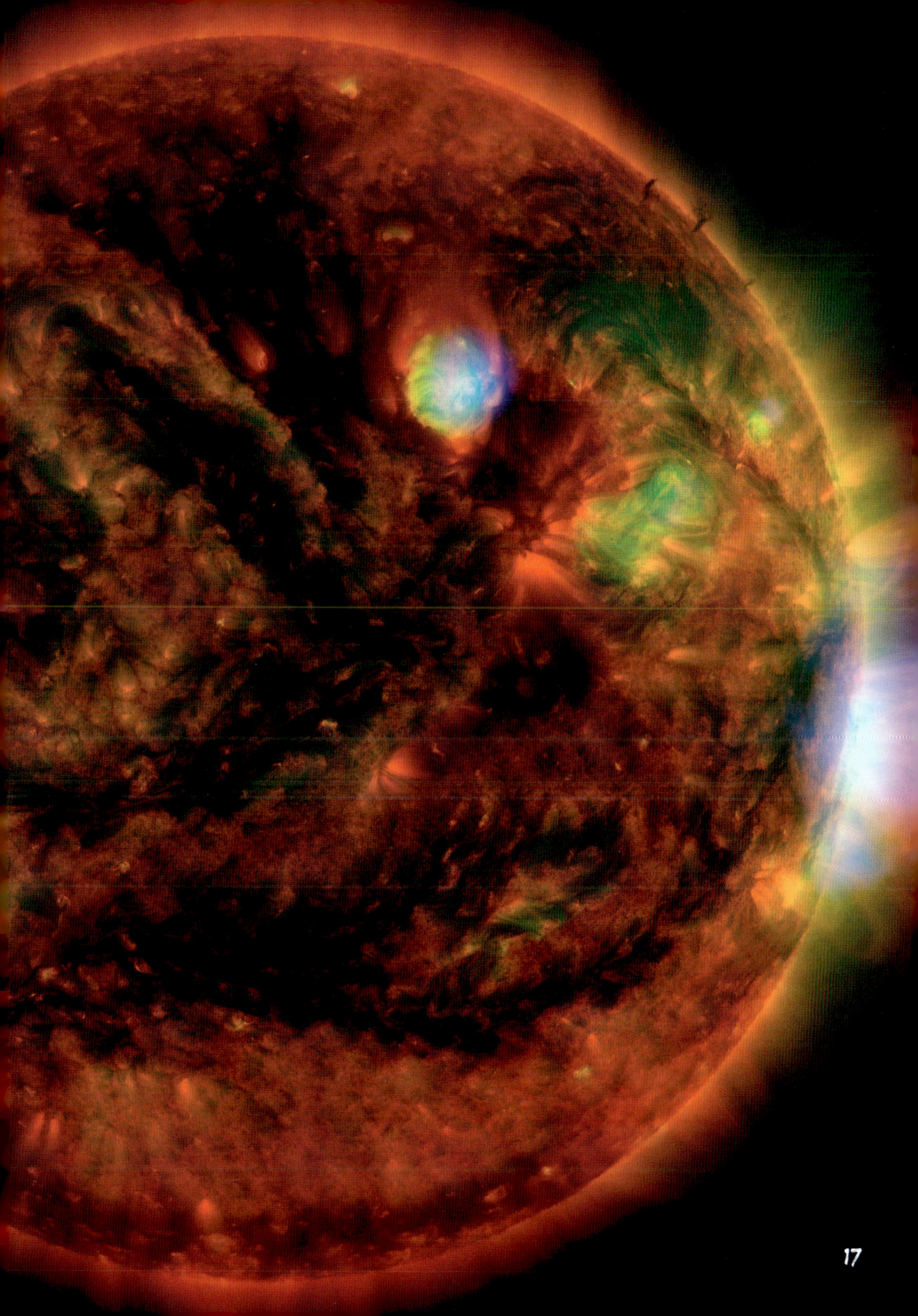

Massive stars are at least 8 times bigger than the sun. These explode into supernovas. Most stars that are 8 to 20 times bigger than the sun then become neutron stars.

And many stars more than 20 times the size of the sun become black holes. This is an area of space with such strong gravity that nothing can escape once pulled in.

Astronomers first observed Kepler's supernova in 1604. It is one of the most recent supernovas in the Milky Way galaxy.

XTREME FACT

Some stars are 1,000 times bigger than the sun!

CHAPTER 5

NEUTRON STARS

A neutron star is the leftover center of a star that exploded. It's not very big. Most neutron stars are about 12 miles (19 km) wide. However, they have a high mass. They also have a very strong pull of gravity. This makes them **extremely dense**.

The Crab Nebula's neutron star. A neutron star is so dense that a spoonful of its matter would weigh 10 million tons (9 million metric tons)!

When two neutron stars crash into each other, the explosion is called a kilonova.

Sometimes two neutron stars crash into each other. They combine to form a bigger neutron star called a magnetar. These stars have very strong magnetic fields. Magnetars can also be very hot. They can reach 18 million degrees Fahrenheit (10 million°C)!

XTREME FACT

Astronomers believe there could be as many as one billion neutron stars in the Milky Way galaxy.

CHAPTER 6

WOLF-RAYET STARS

Stars that are at least 20 times bigger than the sun may become Wolf-Rayet stars. This is the last stage that many huge stars go through before becoming supernovas. Stars in this stage can be hotter than 90,000 degrees Fahrenheit (50,000°C).

XTREME FACT

One of the hottest Wolf-Rayet stars is called WR 102. It is 377,540 degrees Fahrenheit (209,727°C).

Wolf-Rayet star WR 124. French astronomers Charles-Joseph-Étienne Wolf and Georges-Antoine-Pons Rayet discovered Wolf-Rayet stars in 1867.

Wolf-Rayet stars are also known for their very strong **stellar** winds. The great heat and strong winds cause them to quickly burn up and lose their mass. So, most Wolf-Rayet stars only live for a few hundred thousand years. Then they usually explode in a supernova.

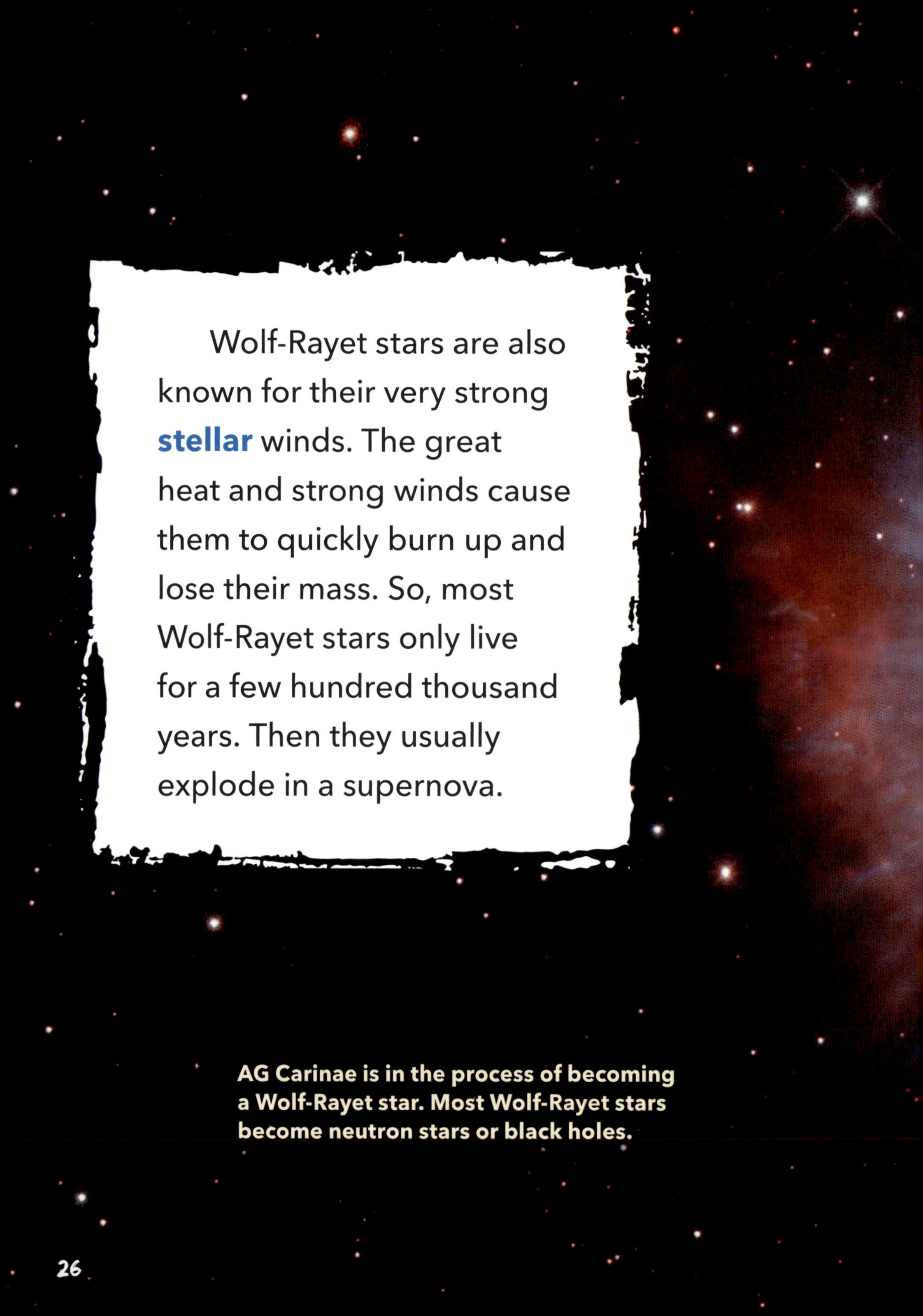

AG Carinae is in the process of becoming a Wolf-Rayet star. Most Wolf-Rayet stars become neutron stars or black holes.

CHAPTER 7

OBSERVING SUPERNOVAS

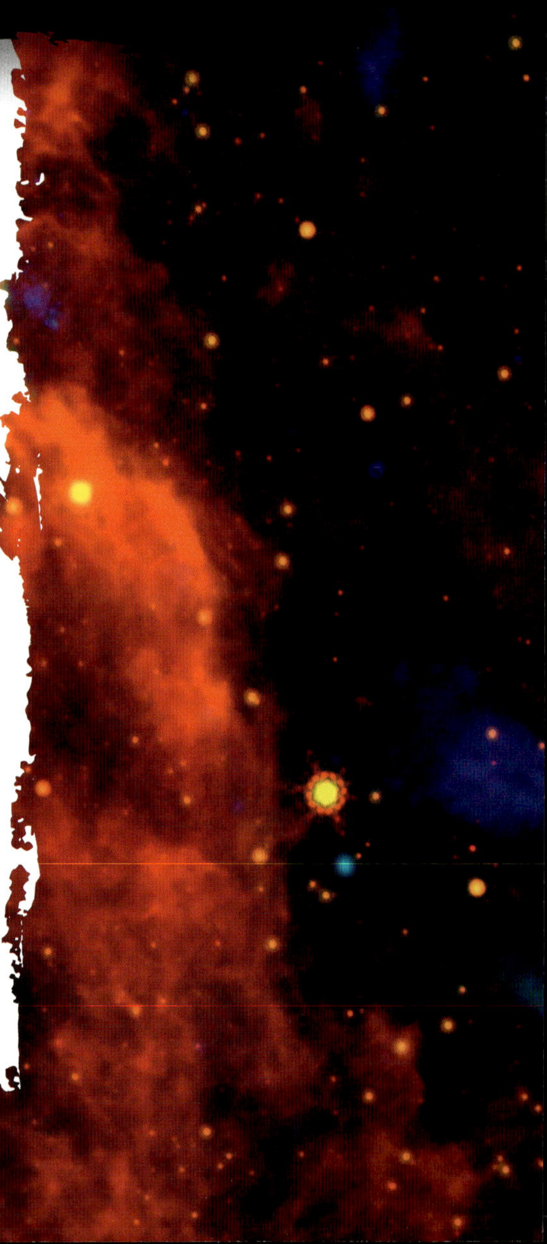

Supernovas within our **galaxy** can often be seen without a telescope. Many ancient astronomers thought supernovas were new stars. This belief continued for hundreds of years.

Modern astronomers know that supernovas are stars at the end of their life. They were simply not bright enough to see until they exploded.

XTREME FACT

There are only two or three supernovas in the Milky Way galaxy every one hundred years.

Chinese astronomers first recorded the appearance of what they thought was a new star in 185 CE. But it is actually the oldest recorded supernova, called RCW 86.

Modern scientists know more about supernovas because of astronomers Walter Baade and Fritz Zwicky. In the 1930s, they identified and explained supernovas. They created the **theory** that supernovas are **collapsing** stars that become neutron stars.

Baade and Zwicky used the telescope at the Mount Wilson Observatory in California to study supernovas.

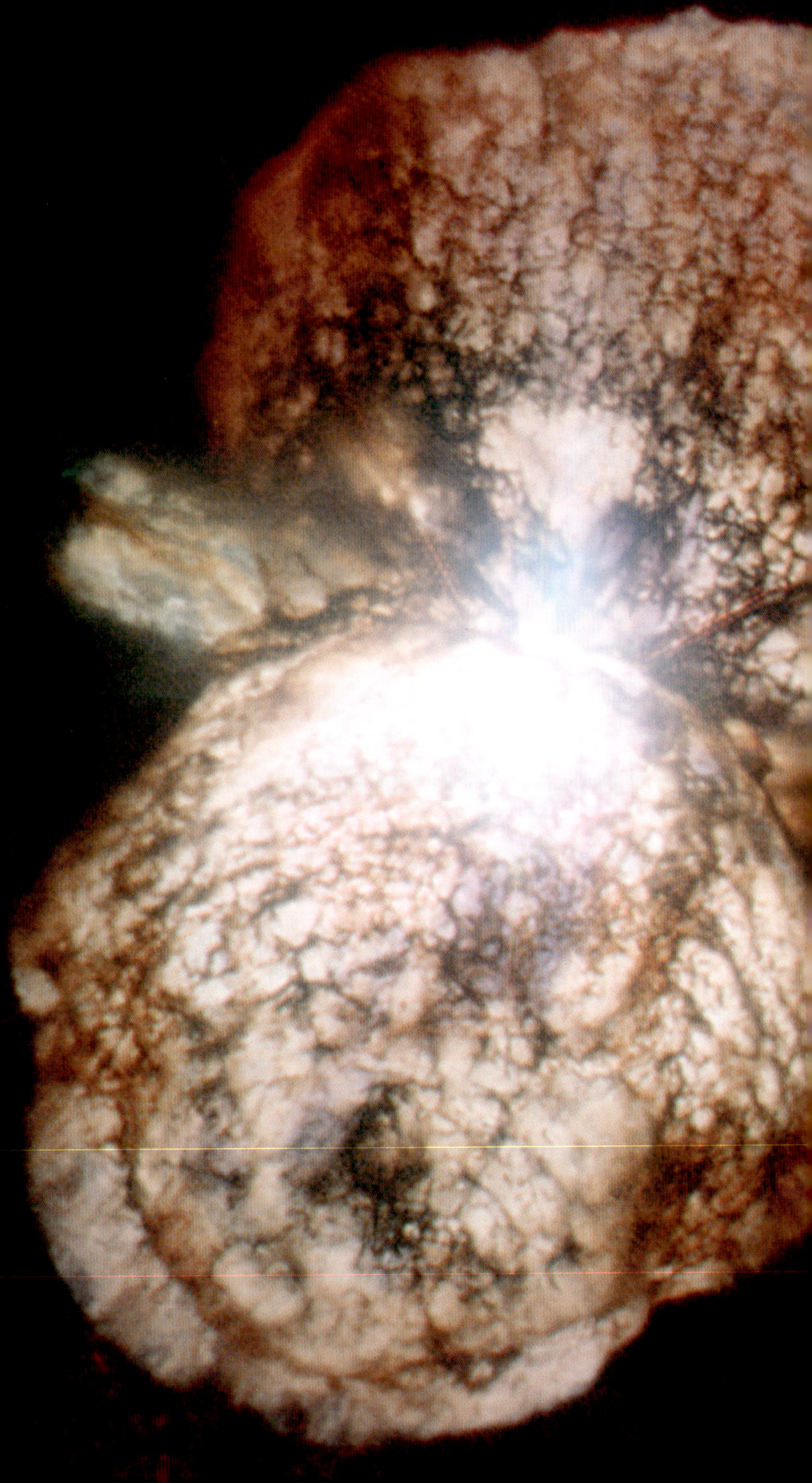

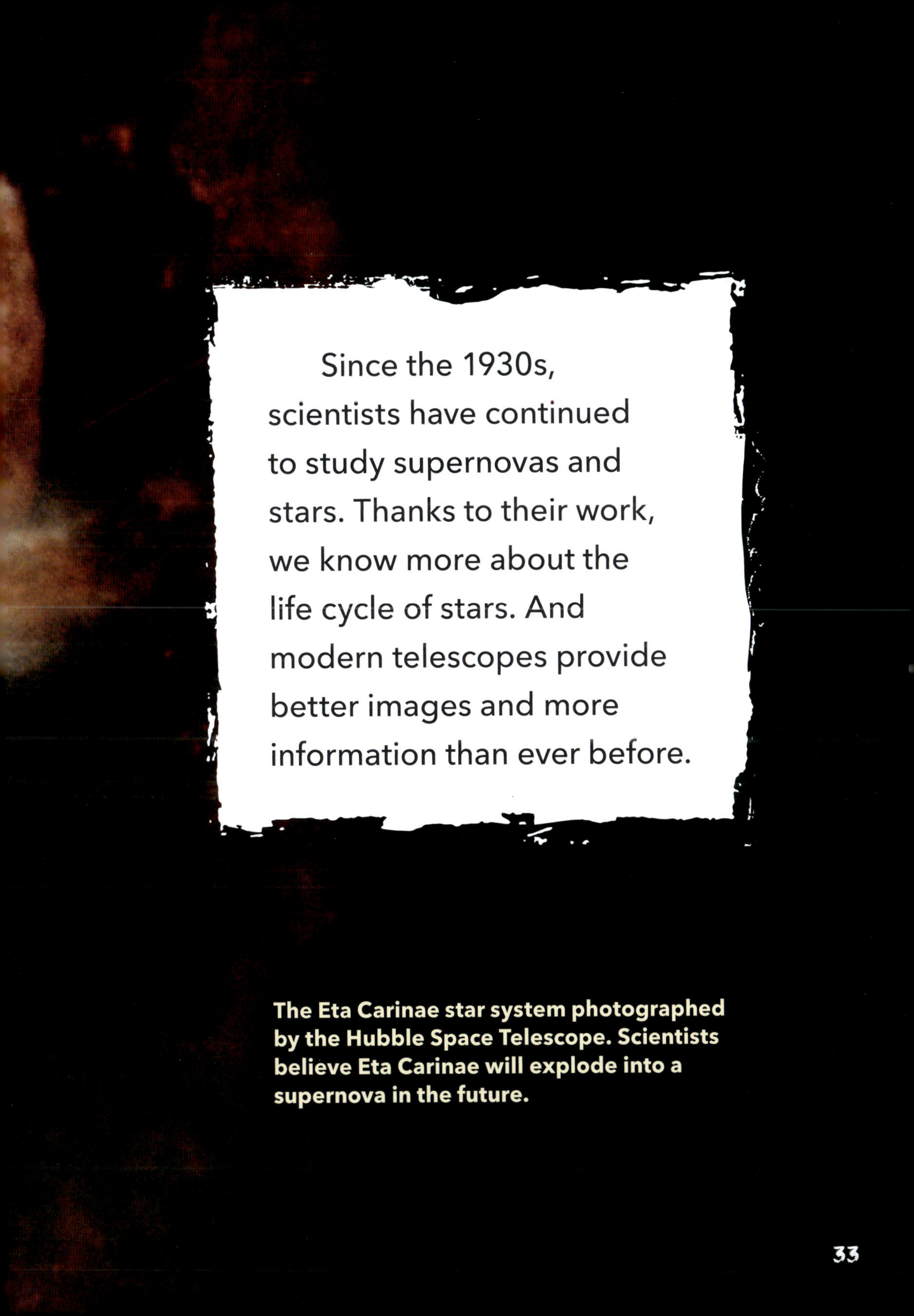

Since the 1930s, scientists have continued to study supernovas and stars. Thanks to their work, we know more about the life cycle of stars. And modern telescopes provide better images and more information than ever before.

The Eta Carinae star system photographed by the Hubble Space Telescope. Scientists believe Eta Carinae will explode into a supernova in the future.

CHAPTER 8

HEAT IN THE LAB

Supernovas and neutron stars are the hottest naturally occurring objects in the universe. However, scientists have measured even hotter temperatures in laboratories.

They use special machines called **ion colliders**. Ions in these machines move almost as fast as light. They also crash into one another. The **collisions** release enormous amounts of energy.

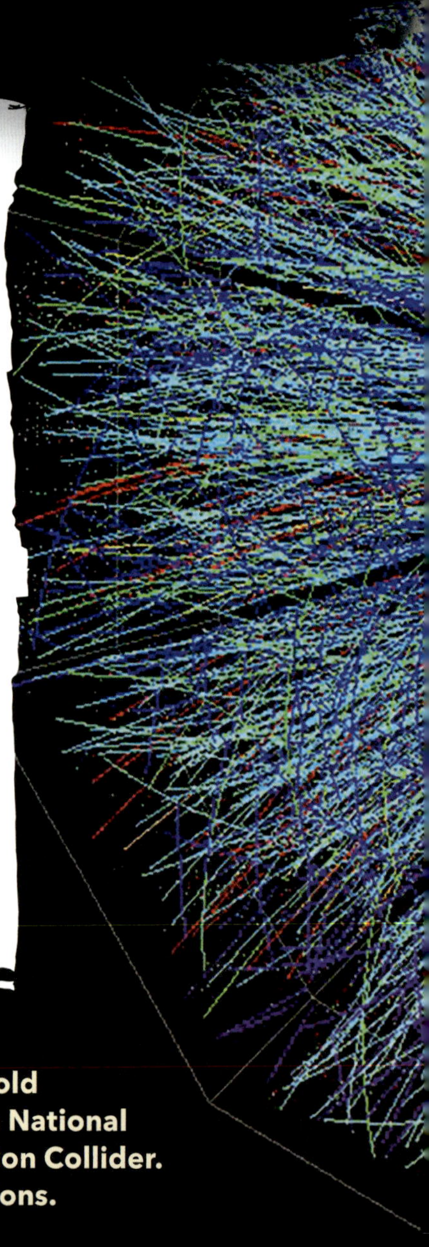

A three-dimensional image of gold ions colliding in the Brookhaven National Laboratory's Relativistic Heavy Ion Collider. The lines show the paths of the ions.

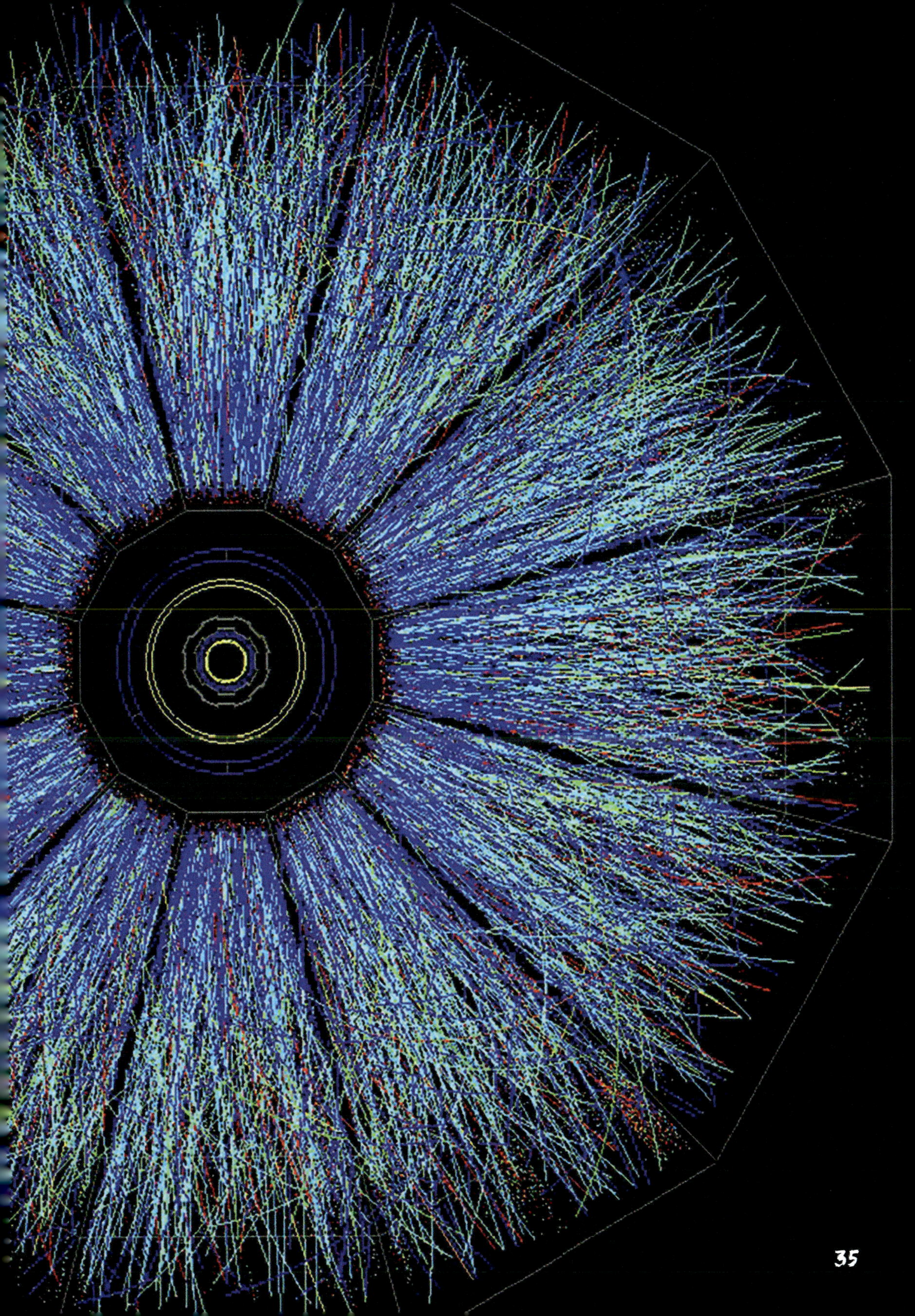

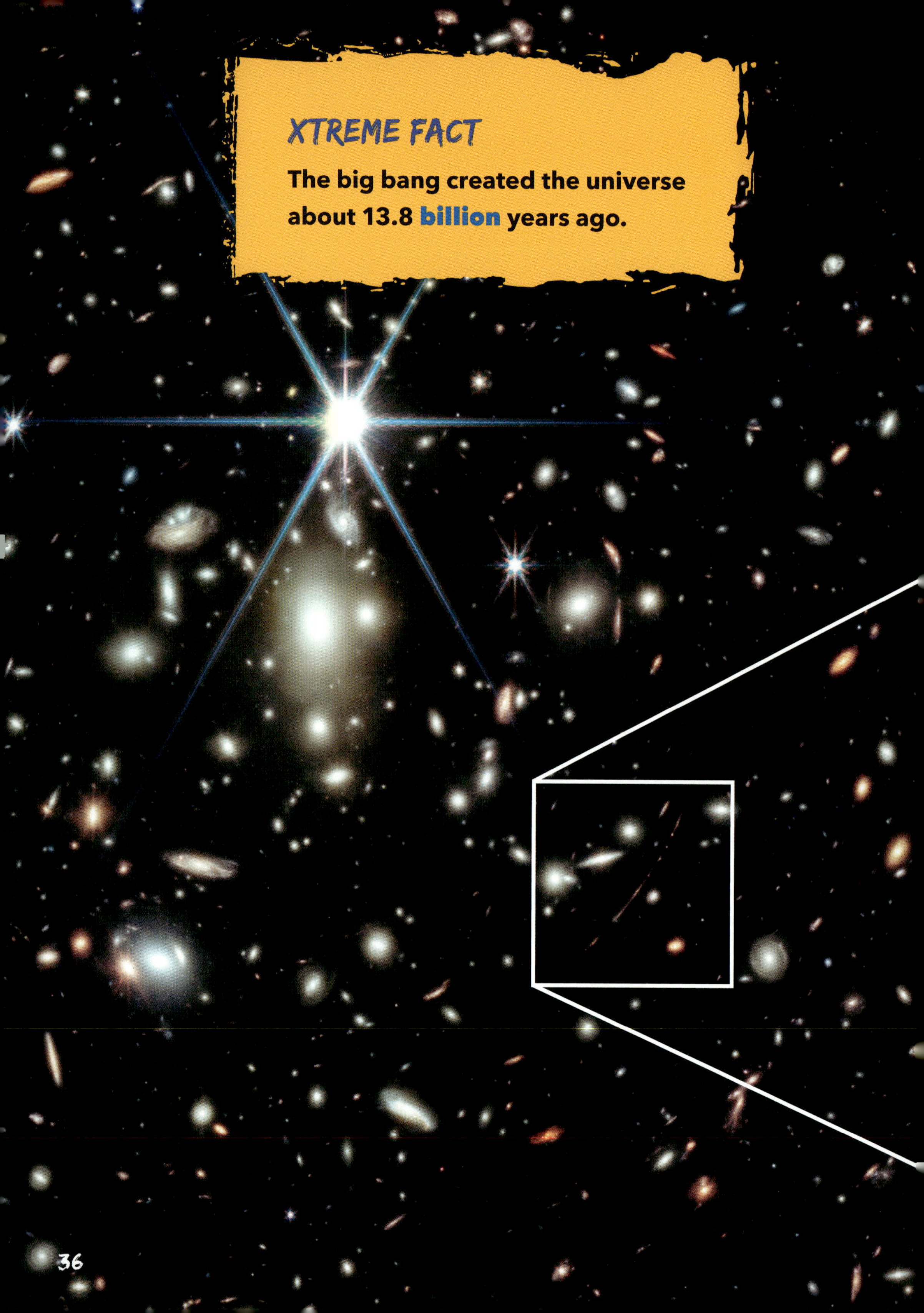

XTREME FACT

The big bang created the universe about 13.8 billion years ago.

The **ion collisions** create a type of matter called **plasma**. For a split second, this plasma is the hottest thing in the universe. But the plasma cools quickly.

Scientists believe plasma was the first type of matter to fill the universe. This would have happened right after the **big bang**. The plasma then cooled and all other types of matter formed.

In 2022, astronomers found one of the most distant stars in the universe. They called it Earendel. It formed in the first billion years after the big bang.

There are two well-known **colliders**. The first is the Relativistic Heavy **Ion** Collider at the Brookhaven National Laboratory in Upton, New York. The second is the Large Hadron Collider (LHC) at CERN in Geneva, Switzerland. Ion **collisions** in both labs have produced temperatures hotter than 7 **trillion** degrees Fahrenheit (4 trillion°C)!

The LHC is one of the most powerful colliders ever built. It is 328 feet (100 m) underground. The collider ring is 16.8 miles (27 km) long.

CHAPTER 9

HEAT ON EARTH

While nowhere near as hot as supernovas or **plasma**, some parts of Earth are superhot. The hottest part of Earth is its inner **core**. The core's temperature ranges from about 8,000 to 10,800 degrees Fahrenheit (4,400 to 6,000°C).

Earth's core is made of mostly nickel and iron.

Scientists use specialized instruments to study Earth's surface temperatures. These instruments are located on spacecraft, such as the Aqua spacecraft.

There are also some very hot places on Earth's surface. One of them is Death Valley in the Mojave Desert in California. In July 1913, temperatures there reached 134 degrees Fahrenheit (57°C).

Then, during a study that lasted from 2002 to 2019, scientists found two locations with an even hotter surface temperature. They recorded a temperature of 177 degrees Fahrenheit (81°C) in the Lut Desert in Iran and the Sonoran Desert in Mexico.

CHAPTER 10

HOT AND FIERY

There are many **extremely** hot things in the universe. These include supernovas, neutron stars, and **plasma** made in labs. Scientists believe these all hold clues to what the universe was like when it first formed. These clues help scientists learn how the universe might change in the future.

Cassiopeia A supernova remnant

XTREME CHALLENGE

TAKE THE QUIZ BELOW AND PUT WHAT YOU'VE LEARNED TO THE TEST!

1) What is a supernova?

2) What kind of chemical reaction happens in a star's core?

3) What did early astronomers think supernovas were?

4) What are some of the stages of a star's life?

5) Where is the hottest place you've ever been?

GLOSSARY

big bang–the explosion that created the universe.

billion–the number 1,000,000,000, or one thousand million.

collapse–to suddenly break down or to cave in.

collide–to come together with force. An act or instance of colliding is a collision.

collider–a machine in which particles, or small pieces of matter, move in opposite directions so that they crash into each other.

core–the center of a space object such as a planet, moon, or star.

dense–having parts very close together.

extremely–to a degree that exceeds the ordinary or expected.

galaxy–a very large group of stars, planets, and other objects in space.

hydrogen–a gas with no smell or color that is lighter than air and catches fire easily.

ion–an atom that has gained or lost electrons.

massive—large and heavy.

outer—located away from a center or inside.

plasma—a type of matter that is similar to a gas but can carry electricity.

reaction—the chemical action of two or more substances on each other. This produces at least one additional substance.

stellar—related to the stars.

theory—a general rule offered to explain a scientific event.

trillion—the number 1,000,000,000,000, or one thousand billion.

ONLINE RESOURCES

Booklinks
NONFICTION NETWORK
FREE! ONLINE NONFICTION RESOURCES

To learn more about supernovas, please visit **abdobooklinks.com** or scan this QR code. These links are routinely monitored and updated to provide the most current information available.

INDEX